Lace
Christmas cards

Gerda Perik

FORTE PUBLISHERS

Contents

Second printing January 2003
ISBN 90 5877 205 5

This is a publication from
Forte Publishers BV
P.O. Box 1394
3500 BJ Utrecht
The Netherlands

For more information about the creative books available from Forte Uitgevers:
www.hobby-party.com

Publisher: Marianne Perlot
Editor: Hanny Vlaar
Photography and digital image editing: Fotografie Gerhard Witteveen, Apeldoorn, the Netherlands
Cover and inner design:
Studio Herman Bade BV, Baarn, the Netherlands

Preface

This is the third Lacé book. The first two books contained cards for every occasion. This book only contains Christmas cards which have been made using the existing templates.

I often hear that people start making Christmas cards during the summer. Personally, I always start too late. Last year, I only started making the card for my granddaughter Merel on time. For her, I made a mother-of-pearl and pink Lacé Christmas card, which still hangs in her bedroom. For this reason, there is a special chapter with baby Christmas cards for all those who are, or will be, a grandmother or grandfather. I have also tried to use many different types of paper in as any different colours as possible. I hope that this book gives you enough inspiration to make attractive Christmas cards.

Good luck!

Gerda

I would like to thank my daughter Mariëlle for helping with the text and Dini Wissink for all the cutting. Thanks!

Techniques

Cutting the Lacé border

The pattern to be cut out is shown on the light green Lacé templates. I prefer to use the attractive Lacé duo-colour paper, which is available in various attractive colour combinations.

Stick the template in the correct position on the card using non-permanent adhesive tape (or Leukopor).

Use the Lacé knife to cut through the openings: start at the point and cut towards the side. Always use a knife with a sharp point. Once you have cut all the lines, carefully remove the template from the card.

It is important to first score the borders that are going to be folded using a Lacé scoring and folding tool.

Next, fold the scored edges towards you and fold them under the points that you have not scored. You will now see the other side of the paper. Since the colours on both sides of the paper compliment each other, you will always be left with a pretty result.

Tip 1
It is easier for right-handed people to cut the template with the word Lacé at the top and for left-handed people to cut the template with the word Lacé at the bottom.

Tip 2:
Rotate the card when cutting a round pattern, so that you do not have to remove your knife from the paper.

Sponging

Dip a cotton bud on an inkpad and brush it over the Lacé borders to give a nice shadow effect.

Copying the star patterns

Copy the star patterns (exact size) using a light box or tracing paper. Stick them on card and cut them out to make templates which you can draw around.

3D cutting

Various cutting patterns are included, but if you use other pictures, carry out the following. Cut out the whole picture for the 1st layer and stick it on the card. For the 2nd layer, do not cut out what is in the background. For the 3rd layer, only cut out what is in the foreground. Puff up the pictures using a shaping pen or your finger and stick them on the card using 3D glue. Place small drops of 3D glue on the back of the pictures and carefully place them in the correct place on top of each other. Press them down carefully, but do not press too hard because you will lose the distance between the various layers.

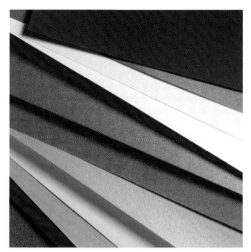

1. Different colours of Lacé duo-colour paper

2. Cut holographic paper to size and stick in on the inside of the card.

3. Cut, score and fold the Lacé border.

4. Finish the card.

Materials

- ❏ Card in Christmas colours (Artoz) and gold card
- ❏ Lacé duo-colour paper: mother-of-pearl and various metallic colours
- ❏ Lacé templates 1 to 21
- ❏ Lacé cutting knife
- ❏ Lacé scoring and folding tool
- ❏ Lacé ruler with a metal cutting edge
- ❏ Glitter glue: transparent and red (Duncan)
- ❏ Cutting sheets by Marianne Design, Picturel and Marjoleine

- ❏ Christmas cutting sheets (50 x 70 cm) (Atelier Barbestyn)
- ❏ Self-adhesive holographic paper: blue, green, red, gold and silver
- ❏ Origami paper: red and blue
- ❏ Stickers: texts, lines and stars
- ❏ Distance punches: Star and small circle
- ❏ Hand punches: Star and small circle (Fiskars)
- ❏ Various punches, including ice-crystal and corner rounder c

- ❏ Various ribbons: red, white and gold
- ❏ Circle cutter
- ❏ 3D glue/silicon glue
- ❏ Photo glue
- ❏ Double-sided adhesive tape
- ❏ Beads and star sequins
- ❏ Non-permanent adhesive tape
- ❏ Scissors
- ❏ Cutting mat and knife
- ❏ Transparent ruler with a metal cutting edge
- ❏ True snow and ultra-fine glitter

Lantern

Mother-of-pearl blue/white duo-colour paper
- *Robed angel cutting sheet* • *White ribbon*
- *Stickers* • *Lacé templates no. 9 and no. 10*

Use the Lacé templates alternately to cut borders every 3.5 cm. Make holes in the short sides and thread them together using a ribbon.

Decorate the lantern with pictures and stars.

Christmas blues

Lantern
cutting
pattern

Star A
Fold line

Use mother-of-pearl blue/white duo-colour paper for these double cards. Make the pictures (Picturel) 3D according to the cutting pattern (or see Techniques). Decorate the cards with stickers.

Card 1

Double card (15 x 15 cm) • White card (7 x 7 cm)
• Lacé template no. 19
Cut two 6 cm long diagonal lines in the front of the card which cross each other in the middle. Fold the flaps over. Cut grooves in the card and stick the points in them. Cut four Lacé borders and cut off the corners at an angle. Stick the white square and the picture on the inside of the card.

Card 2

Duo-colour paper (double card 14 x 14 cm and Ø 3.8 cm)
• Card: white (12 x 12 cm) and blue (Ø 9 cm) • Gold card (Ø 4 cm) • Circle cutter • Lacé template no. 13
Cut a circle out of the card (Ø 9 cm). Cut out the Lacé border in the circle and stick this circle and the blue circle in the card. Stick the small circles on the card. Cut a circle (Ø 9 cm) out of the middle of the white card and cut the piece that remains into four. Punch out stars and stick everything together.

Card 3

Double card (15 x 15 cm) • Card: purple (5.2 x 5.2 cm) and blue (5 x 5 cm) • Rounder c punch • Lacé template no. 21
See card 1, but cut two horizontal lines of 5.5 cm. Stick the purple and blue squares (punch out the corners) in the card.

Card 4

Card (29.7 x 14.8 cm) • Card: silver (13.5 x 10 cm), white (12.5 x 9 cm) and blue (13 x 9.5 cm and

14.8 x 4.5 cm) • Star hand punch • Lacé template no. 1
Score the card 5.5 cm from the left-hand side
(cut the Lacé border out of this strip and stick
the blue strip behind it) and 12 cm from the
right-hand side. Fold the card into shape. Punch
stars out of the white strip and stick the other
layers on top of each other.

Card 5
*Duo-colour paper (double card 14 x 14 cm and
13 x 13 cm) • Gold card (Ø 4.5 cm) • Star hand punch
• Rounder c punch • Lacé template no. 12*
Punch out the corners of the white square. Cut
a circle (Ø 4.8 cm) out of the middle and make
the piece that you cut out smaller (Ø 4.3 cm).
Draw lines to help you and cut out the Lacé
border. Stick the small circles on the card.

Card 6
*Duo-colour paper (double card 14 x 14 cm and a
scrap piece) • Blue card for the star (C) and a circle*

*(Ø 5.8 cm) • Star hand
punch • Glitter glue •
Lacé template no. 17*
Cut out a blue and
a white star (see
page 23). Cut the
Lacé border out of
the white star and
punch stars out of it.
Stick everything on
the card as shown in
the photograph.
Add glitter glue to
the picture.

Gift labels
These are made
using scrap pieces
of paper and Lacé
templates no. 18
and no. 19.

Holly and Christmas decorations

Use red (Artoz 517) and green (Artoz 309) card for the double cards. Christmas cutting sheets with holly (Atelier Barbestyn) are used for the background. Make the pictures (Marianne Design) 3D (or see Techniques). Sponge the Lacé borders (see Techniques) and decorate the cards with stickers.

Card 1

Green card (double card 14.8 x 10.5 cm and Ø 3.8 cm)
• *Mother-of-pearl pastel green/white duo-colour paper*
• *Gold card (5 x 5 cm and Ø 2.5 cm)* • *Gold holographic paper* • *Eyelet and ribbon* • *Lacé template no. 13*
Cut the Lacé border out of a pastel green circle (Ø 9 cm). Do not cut out the last 1.5 cm of the circumference, but make a hanging loop and push an eyelet through it. Stick holographic paper behind the circle and fix the Christmas ball to the card using a ribbon. Sponge the edge of the green circle and stick everything together as shown in the photograph.

Card 2

Green card (double card 14.8 x 10.5 cm and 14.8 x 3.5 cm) • *Gold card (14.8 x 4 cm)* • *Christmas cutting sheet (14.8 x 10.5 cm)* • *Red glitter glue* • *Lacé template no. 9*

Stick the Christmas cutting sheet on the card. Cut the Lacé border out of the green strip and stick the gold card behind it.
Sponge the points which have been folded over. Stick a holly leaf from the Christmas cutting sheet on the card. Make it 3D and add glitter glue to it.

Card 3

Red card (double card 14.8 x 10.5 cm and 14.8 x 3.5 cm) • *Gold card (14.8 x 4 cm)* • *Christmas cutting sheet (14.8 x 10.5 cm)* • *Ribbon* • *Lacé template no. 10*
Stick the Christmas cutting sheet on the card. Cut the Lacé border out of the red strip. Sponge the points which have been folded over and thread a ribbon through them. Stick the gold card behind it. Make a couple of holly branches 3D.

Card 4

Red card (double card 14 x 14 cm and Ø 9 cm) • *Green card (Ø 11 cm)* • *Gold card (13.5 x 13.5 cm and Ø 8.7 cm)* • *Christmas cutting sheet (13 x 13 cm)* • *Ribbon* • *Small circle hand punch* • *Lacé template no. 13*
Cut the Lacé border out of the red circle. Stick the gold card behind it and sponge the points which have been folded over. Punch holes in the green circle every 2 cm and thread the ribbon through them.

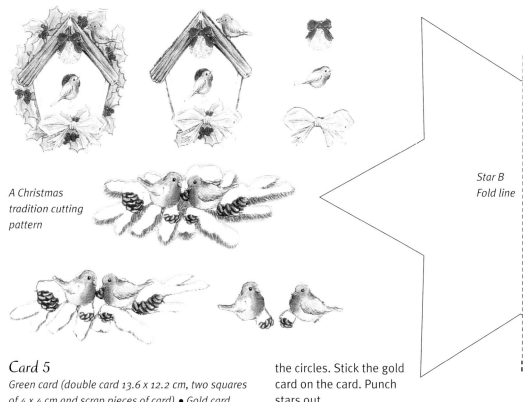

A Christmas tradition cutting pattern

Star B
Fold line

Card 5

Green card (double card 13.6 x 12.2 cm, two squares of 4 x 4 cm and scrap pieces of card) • Gold card (13 x 11.5 cm and two squares of 5 x 5 cm) • Star and small circle hand punches • Green holographic paper (two Ø 4.5 cm) • Red ribbons • Red Identi-pen • Lacé template no. 17

Cut the Lacé border out of two green circles (Ø 4.8 cm), but do not cut out the last 1.5 cm of the circumference. Cut out a hanging loop here and stick the holographic paper behind the circles. Stick the gold card on the card. Punch stars out

Card 6

Green card (double card 13 x 13 cm and Ø 9 cm) • Gold card (12 x 12 cm and Ø 9.5 cm) • Christmas cutting sheet (11.5 x 11.5 cm) • Lacé template no. 3

Cut the Lacé border out of the green circle. Sponge the points which have been folded over and stick everything on the card.

1.

2.

3.

4.

5.

6.

A Christmas tradition

Use red (Artoz 517) and green (Artoz 309) card and self-adhesive gold holographic paper for the double cards (14.8 x 10.5 cm). Make the pictures (Marianne Design) 3D according to the cutting pattern or see Techniques. Decorate the cards with stickers.

Card 1

Green double card • Red A4 card • Gold card (14.8 x 3.8 cm) • Red glitter glue • Lacé template no. 9

Cut out a red circle (Ø 13 cm) and, from this, cut out two circles (Ø 12.5 cm and Ø 12 cm). Cut the circle and the borders in half. Save the scrap pieces of card for card 3. Cut the Lacé border out of a red strip (14.8 x 3.5 cm) and stick gold card behind it. Stick the semicircle and the largest half circumference on the card. Add glitter glue to the picture.

Card 2

Red double card • Green card (14.8 x 10.5 cm and Ø 9 cm) • Gold card (Ø 3.5 cm) • Gold holographic paper (twice Ø 8.5 cm) • Lacé template no. 6

On the green card, cut two diagonal lines (not all the way through the middle) and cut a strip (3 mm) from the slanting edges. Stick the holographic paper against the green circle. Cut out the Lacé border and stick holographic paper behind it.

Card 3

Green double card • Red card • Gold card (Ø 5 cm) • Gold holographic paper (14.8 x 9 cm and Ø 4.3 cm) • Star hand punch • Lacé template no. 17

Use the scrap pieces of card from card 1. Cut the piece left over from cutting the circle so that it is 3 cm wide. Punch out stars and stick holographic paper behind it. Cut a 3 mm wide red strip. Stick the holographic paper behind the red card (Ø 4.5 cm) and cut out the Lacé border.

Card 4

Red card (double card and 11.5 x 7 cm) • Green card (12.5 x 8 cm) • Gold holographic paper • Lacé template no. 19

Cut a corner strip (1 cm wide) from the right-hand side of the green card and cut the corners at an angle. Cut a corner strip (2 cm wide) from the left-hand side of the red rectangle and stick holographic paper behind it. Cut the Lacé border out of this corner strip.

Gift label

Make this card using scrap pieces of paper and Lacé template no. 17. Sponge the Lacé borders (see Techniques).

Baby's Christmas cutting pattern

Baby's Christmas

Use different colours of mother-of-pearl duo-colour paper for the double card (14.8 x 10.5 cm). Make the pictures (robed angel cutting sheet) 3D according to the cutting pattern (also see page 32). Decorate the cards with stickers.

Card 1

Pastel pink/white duo-colour paper (double card and Ø 8.8 cm) • Old rose/white duo-colour paper (Ø 9 cm) • Lacé template no. 13
Cut the Lacé border out of the pastel pink circle and stick the old rose card behind it.

Card 2

Green/white duo-colour paper (double card, Ø 9 cm and Ø 3 cm) • Pastel green/white duo-colour paper (Ø 9.2 cm and Ø 4 cm) • Letter punch • Lacé template no. 6
Cut the Lacé border out of the green circle and stick the large pastel green card behind it. Cut the small circles into four and stick them in the corners.
Punch out the letters and stick them on the card.

Card 3

Orange/white duo-colour paper (double card, 7.5 x 7.5 cm and 7 x 7 cm) • White card (7.3 x 7.3 cm) • Lacé template no. 9

Cut a part of the Lacé border out of the small orange square and fold over the corners. Stick this on white card and then on the large orange square.

Card 4

Blue/white duo-colour card • Lacé template no. 2
Open the card and cut the Lacé border out of the top and bottom edge, approximately 1 cm from the edge of the card.

Card 5

Old rose/white duo-colour paper (14.8 x 29.4 cm) • Letter punch • Lacé template no. 10
Divide the card into three. Cut the Lacé border in the folds of the card. Fold one flap inwards. Punch out the letters and stick them on the card.

Card 6

Pastel blue/white duo-colour paper (double card and Ø 9 cm) • Blue/white duo-colour paper (Ø 9 cm) • Star sequins • Blue beads • Needle and thread • Lace template no. 3
Cut the Lacé border out of the pastel blue circle and cut it out as shown in the photograph. Weave the points together and embroider the stars and beads on them. Stick the blue circle behind it.

Gift labels
These are made using scrap pieces of paper and Lacé templates no. 17 and no. 18.

Blue variations

Use dark blue card (Artoz 417) and mother-of-pearl pastel blue/white duo-colour paper for the double cards. Make the pictures 3D according to the cutting pattern. Decorate the cards with stickers.

Card 1

Blue card (double card 15 x 15 cm and 12 x 12 cm)
• Duo-colour paper • Silver holographic paper
(12.5 x 12.5 cm and 10 x 10 cm) • Rounder c punch
• Lacé template no. 17

Stick the small piece of holographic paper behind the small blue square. Cut all the template's Lacé borders out. Stick the large piece of holographic paper behind the blue square. Stick pastel blue frames (4.7 x 4.7 and 2 mm wide) with punched out corners around the Lacé borders. Make two grooves in the bottom left-hand and top right-hand corners 3 cm from the corners and 2 cm from the edge. Slide the blue square (12 x 12 cm) in these grooves.

Card 2

Blue card (double card 22 x 14.8 cm and 14.8 x 3.5 cm)
• Silver holographic paper (14.8 x 4 cm) • Picturel
cutting sheet • True snow and ultra-fine glitter • Circle
cutter • Lacé template no. 10

Score the card 5.5 cm from the sides. Fold the card and round off the top of the card using the circle cutter (Ø 11 cm). Cut the Lacé border out of the blue strip and stick the holographic paper behind it. Stick this on the card and cut the border to size. Finish the picture using True snow and sprinkle fine glitter on it.

Card 3

Blue card (double card 14.8 x 10.5 cm and Ø 4 cm) •
Duo-colour paper (14.5 x 10 cm) • Reuser Christmas
punch • Blue holographic paper (Ø 9 cm and scrap
pieces) • Marianne Design cutting sheet • Glitter
glue • Split pin • Lacé template no. 4

Cut the Lacé template out of the duo-colour paper. Punch out the corners and stick blue ice-crystals on the card. Stick the cards together using a split pin. Stick the holographic paper circle in the double card behind the cut out border and stick the small circle on it.

Card 4

*Blue card (double card 14.8 x 10.5 cm and
Ø 9 cm) • Self-adhesive silver holographic paper
(Ø 9.5 cm and Ø 9 cm) • Pictureel cutting sheet
• Lacé template no. 13*

Stick the small circle of holographic paper behind
the blue circle and cut the Lacé border out of it.
Cut out the pattern leaving a 2 mm border. Stick
it on the large circle of holographic paper and cut
out the pattern leaving a 2 mm border.

Card 5

*Duo-colour paper (double card 14.8 x 10.5 cm and
14.8 x 3.5 cm) • Blue card (14.8 x 4.5 cm) • Reuser*
*Christmas punch • Sequins and blue beads
• Needle and thread • Marianne Design cutting
sheet • Red text sticker • Gold gel pen • Lacé
template no. 2*

Cut the Lacé border out of the pastel blue strip
and embroider the stars and beads to the
points which have been folded over.
Stick the holographic paper behind it. Punch
out the corners of the blue strip. Stick everything on the card and draw lines on the card.

Gift label

Make this card using scrap pieces of paper
and Lacé template no. 19.

BLUE VARIATIONS

Christmas stars

Use blue/silver metallic duo-colour paper for the double cards and the stars. The drawings of the stars are given on pages 7, 11, 23, 26 and 31. Make the pictures (Marianne Design) 3D according to the cutting pattern (or see Techniques). Decorate the cards with stickers.

Card 1

Card: double card 12 x 12 cm, star (A), Ø 3.8 cm and Ø 1.8 cm • Red holographic paper: star (A) and Ø 5 cm • White gel pen • Lacé template no. 17
Stick the stars (page 7) on the card and draw a decorative line around it 2 mm from the star. Cut the Lacé border out of the circle (Ø 3.8 cm) and stick all the circles on top of each other.

Card 2

Card (double card 16.5 x 12 cm, 6 x 2 cm and Ø 3.8 cm) • Red holographic paper (Ø 9 cm) • Small circle hand punch • Red ribbon • Lacé template no. 13
Cut a circle (Ø 9 cm) out of the front of the card. Make holes around the circle every 1.5 cm. Thread a ribbon through the holes and attach a label to the ribbon with a Christmas wish. Cut the Lacé border out of the circle you have cut out and cut around it leaving a 2 mm border. Stick the circle and the red holographic paper inside the card.

Card 3

Duo-colour paper (two large stars (E) and one small star (C) and Ø 4.5 cm) • Red holographic paper for the star and Ø 10 cm • Star hand punch • Red string • Lacé template no. 17
Cut out the large stars (page 31). Punch stars out of the small silver star (page 23) and stick it on the red holographic paper. Cut out the star with a 2 mm border. Stick this star on the blue star and also punch stars out of this. Stick the red circle behind the blue star and then stick everything on the large silver star. Attach the string to two points of the blue star. Cut the Lacé border out of the small circle. Cut around it leaving a 1 mm border and stick the circle in the middle of the stars.

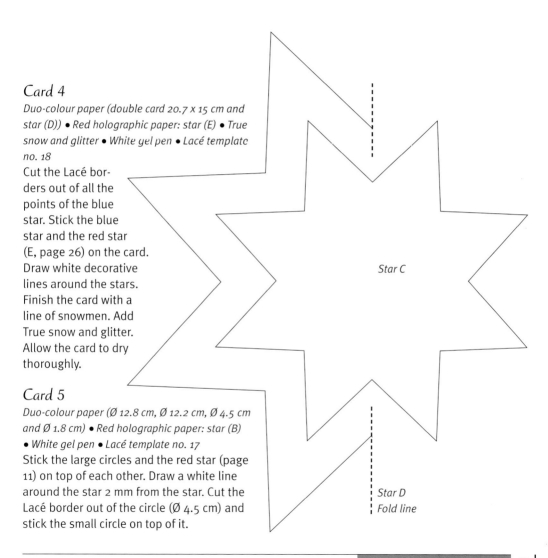

Card 4

Duo-colour paper (double card 20.7 x 15 cm and star (D)) • *Red holographic paper: star (E)* • *True snow and glitter* • *White gel pen* • *Lacé template no. 18*

Cut the Lacé borders out of all the points of the blue star. Stick the blue star and the red star (E, page 26) on the card. Draw white decorative lines around the stars. Finish the card with a line of snowmen. Add True snow and glitter. Allow the card to dry thoroughly.

Card 5

Duo-colour paper (Ø 12.8 cm, Ø 12.2 cm, Ø 4.5 cm and Ø 1.8 cm) • *Red holographic paper: star (B)* • *White gel pen* • *Lacé template no. 17*

Stick the large circles and the red star (page 11) on top of each other. Draw a white line around the star 2 mm from the star. Cut the Lacé border out of the circle (Ø 4.5 cm) and stick the small circle on top of it.

Star C

Star D
Fold line

Shiny gold

Use bronze/gold and ivory/gold (card 2) metallic duo-colour paper for the double cards (14.8 x 10.5 cm and 15 x 15 cm). Make the pictures (Marianne Design and Marjoleine, card 4) 3D (see Techniques). Decorate the cards with stickers and add some glitter glue.

Card 1

Duo-colour paper (double card and 3.5 cm wide strip) • Gold card (14.8 x 3.7 cm) • Romak star frame • Red Identi-pen • Lacé template no. 9
Cut the Lacé border out of the bronze strip and stick the gold card behind it. Colour the points of the stars using the Identi-pen.

Card 2

Duo-colour paper • Bronze/gold duo-colour paper • Gold origami paper • Ribbon • Lacé template no. 6
Cut the Lacé border out of a bronze circle (Ø 9 cm). Do not cut out the last 1.5 cm of the circumference, but make a hanging loop and attach an eyelet to it. Stick the origami paper behind it. Stick the circle and the ribbon on the card.

Card 3

Duo-colour paper (double card and Ø 4.3 cm) • Gold card (Ø 4.5 cm) • Romak star frame • Glitter glue

• Brown Identi-pen • Lacé templates no. 9 and no. 17
Cut the round Lacé border out of the bronze circle and stick the gold card behind it.
Cut out the other Lacé border in the fold of the card.
Put a brown dot in the stars.

Card 4

Duo-colour paper (double card and 13 x 13 cm)
• Red origami paper (13.5 x 13.5 cm) • Gold card (four squares of 3.5 x 3.5 cm) • Rounder c punch • Lacé template no. 10
Draw lines to help you and cut the Lacé border out of the card. Stick the origami paper behind it. Punch out the corners of the small squares and stick them on the card.

Card 5

Duo-colour paper (double card and 13 x 13 cm)
• Gold card (13.5 x 13.5 cm and three circles Ø 4 cm) • Glitter glue • Red Identi-pen • Lacé template no. 13
Cut the half Lacé borders out of the card. Put a red dot in the stars.

Gift label

Make this card using scrap pieces of paper and Lacé template no. 19.

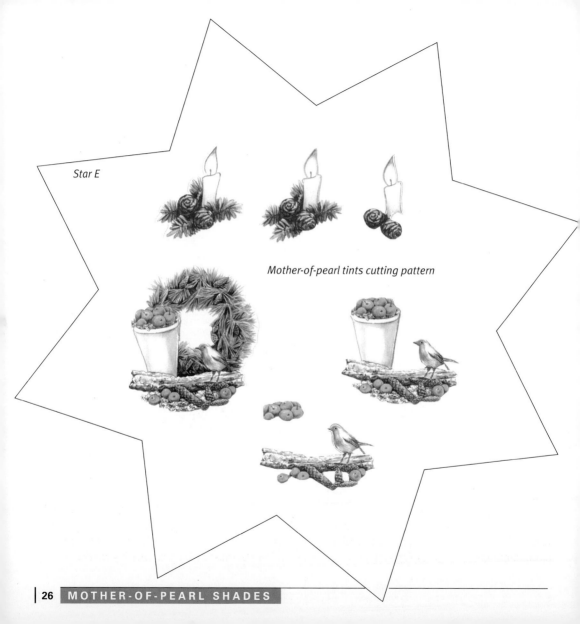

Star E

Mother-of-pearl tints cutting pattern

Mother-of-pearl shades

Use various colours of duo-colour paper and eco-paper with a gold border for the double cards.
Make the pictures (Picturel) 3D according to the cutting pattern (or see Techniques). Decorate the cards with stickers and add some glitter glue.

Card 1

Blue/white duo-colour paper (14.8 x 10.5 cm) • White card (14.8 x 10.5 cm) • Blue eco-paper (14.8 x 10.5 cm and Ø 4 cm) • Aslan • Lacé template no. 13
Draw a diagonal pencil line on the card. Cut a semicircle (Ø 9 cm) half way along the line on the right-hand side and cut the rest of the card away. Cut the Lacé border out of the circle and cut around it leaving a 1 mm border. Stick the eco-paper and the Aslan on the white card and stick this behind the other card. Stick the blue circle and the picture on the card.

Card 2

Pastel pink/white duo-colour paper (double card 14.8 x 10.5 cm) • White card (14.8 x 10.5 cm) Wine red eco-paper (14.8 x 10.5 cm and Ø 4 cm) • Lacé template no. 13
Make this card according to the instructions given for card 1, except do not cut a border along the right-hand part of the circle.

Card 3

Blue/white duo-colour paper (double card 17 x 10.5 cm and Ø 9.5 cm) • Blue eco-paper (10 x 10 cm) • Gold gel pen • Aslan • Lacé template no. 3
First, stick the eco-paper on the Aslan. Cut the Lacé border out of the white circle and cut around it leaving a 3 mm border. Stick it on the eco-paper and cut around the edge leaving a 2 mm border. Next, stick in on the top of the card and cut around it leaving a 2 mm border. Draw a decorative line on the card.

Card 4

Old rose/white duo-colour paper (double card 14 x 14 cm and Ø 9 cm) • Pink eco-paper (Ø 9.3 and two strips of 14 x 2 cm) • Aslan • Lacé template no. 3
First, stick the eco-paper on the Aslan. Cut the Lacé border out of the old rose circle and stick it on the eco-paper circle.

Card 5

Pastel green/white duo-colour paper (double card 14.8 x 10.5 cm) • Eco-paper (two 3 cm wide strips) • Lacé template no. 21
Cut the Lacé border out of the middle of the card. Stick the strips of eco-paper on the left-hand and right-hand sides of the card and make the pictures 3D. Finish the strips with line stickers.

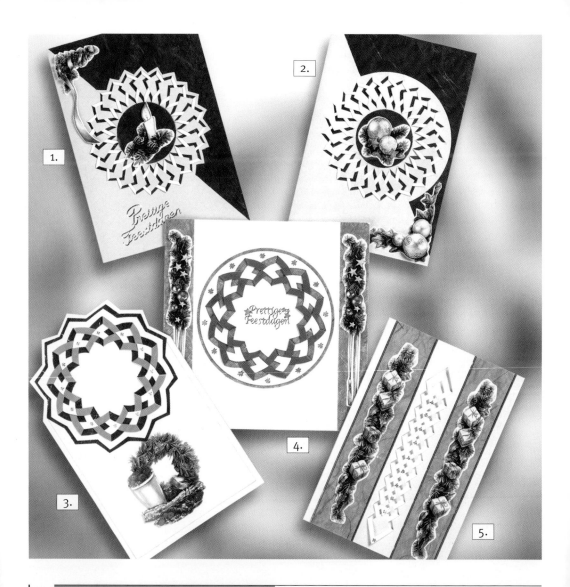

Attractive ivory

Use ivory/gold metallic duo-colour paper for the double cards (14.8 x 10.5 cm and 13 x 13 cm). Make the pictures 3D (see Techniques). Decorate the cards with stickers and add some glitter glue.

Card 1

Duo-colour paper (double card) • Styropor (11.3 x 3.2 cm) • Gold card (11.3 x 3.2 cm) • Eyelet • Border sticker • Shake-it cutting sheet • Lacé template no. 11

Cut out a rectangle (11.5 x 3.5 cm) 1.5 cm from the left-hand side of the card. Cut 1 mm off of all the sides of the strip and cut the Lacé border out of it. First, stick gold card behind it and then stick it on the styropor. Stick everything inside the card so that it fits inside the frame. Stick a border sticker around the frame. Puff up the Christmas decorations and stick them on the card using 3D glue. Attach a thread to them and tie them to the eyelet.

Card 2

Duo-colour paper (double card) • Gold card (11.5 x 11.5 cm frame which is 2 mm wide) • Ornare Christmas cutting sheet • Lacé template no. 3

Cut the Lacé border out of the middle of the card and stick the gold frame around it. Cover the area with poinsettias. Stick some stars on the card using 3D glue.

Card 3

Duo-colour paper (double card) • Blue card (Artoz 425) • Gold card (3.8 x 3.8 cm) • Marianne Design cutting sheet • Lacé template no. 21

Cut a square (4 x 4 cm) out of the middle of the card and stick a blue frame around it which is 0.5 cm bigger. Cut the Lacé borders out parallel to each other. Stick a blue frame (14.3 x 9.5 cm and 0.5 cm wide) on the card. Stick a blue square (4 x 4 cm) on the inside of the card and stick the gold square and the picture on this.

Card 4

Duo-colour paper (double card and 7 x 7 cm) • Gold card (9 x 9 cm) • Blue card (8.5 x 8.5 cm) • Shake-it cutting sheet • Lacé template no. 21

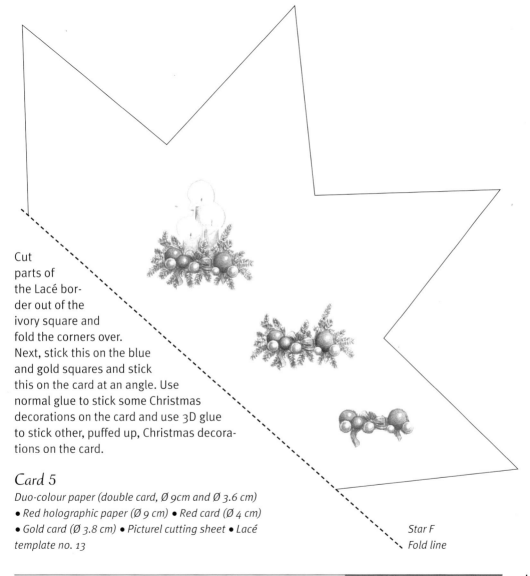

Cut
parts of
the Lacé bor-
der out of the
ivory square and
fold the corners over.
Next, stick this on the blue
and gold squares and stick
this on the card at an angle. Use
normal glue to stick some Christmas
decorations on the card and use 3D glue
to stick other, puffed up, Christmas decorations on the card.

Card 5

Duo-colour paper (double card, Ø 9cm and Ø 3.6 cm)
• Red holographic paper (Ø 9 cm) • Red card (Ø 4 cm)
• Gold card (Ø 3.8 cm) • Picturel cutting sheet • Lacé
template no. 13

Star F
Fold line

Cut the Lacé template out of the largest ivory circle and cut out the pattern leaving a 2 mm wide the border. Stick this on the red holographic paper. Stick all the small circles on the card.

Gift labels

These are made using scrap pieces of paper and Lacé templates no. 17 and no. 20.

*Baby's Christmas
cutting pattern*

Shopkeepers can order the materials from: Kars & Co. B.V. in Ochten, the Netherlands.